Mel Bay Presents

THE CAT'S MEOW

Ukulele Favorites from the Roaring Twenties

Compiled, Written, and Produced by Ian Whitcomb
(with CD Songs Performed by Ian Whitcomb
& His Bungalow Boys)

W9-BQW-496

CD CONTENTS

1. ME-OW! (Tom Marion, banjo solo)
2. I'LL SIT RIGHT ON THE MOON (AND KEEP MY EYES ON YOU) (Dan Levinson's Eleven Sons Of Rosy)
3. YOU'RE IN STYLE WHEN YOU'RE WEARING A SMILE (Dick Zimmerman, piano)
4. ALICE BLUE GOWN
5. SHINE (Dan Levinson, C melody saxophone solo; Tom Marion, guitar solo)
6. BIMINI BAY (Crystal Palace Orchestra)
7. I AIN'T GOT NOBODY MUCH
8. PRETTY BABY
9. DAPPER DAN (FROM DEAR OLD DIXIELAND) (Trevor Crozier & Ian Whitcomb, vocal duet)
10. POOR BUTTERFLY (Crystal Palace Orchestra)
11. I'LL STAND BENEATH YOUR WINDOW (AND WHISTLE)
12. WONDERFUL ONE (Bobby Bruce, violin solo)
13. MARGIE (Dan Levinson, saxophone; Tom Marion, guitar)
14. ANY PLACE WHERE I MAKE MONEY (IS HOME SWEET HOME TO ME) (Martin Jenkins, violin)
15. ALL BY MYSELF (Regina Whitcomb, vocal)
16. THE SHEIK OF ARABY
17. I WAS A FOOL
18. THE DARKTOWN STRUTTERS' BALL
19. THE CANDYLAND CHRISTMAS BALL
20. LONELY (Regina Whitcomb, vocal)
21. WHEN YOU'RE THERE (Regina Whitcomb, vocal)
22. DO I LOVE YOU? YES, I DO ! (Regina & Ian Whitcomb, vocals)
23. DOWN ON THE FARM
24. HELLO! GOOD MORNING! AND HOW DO YOU DO? (Fred Sokolow, vocal)
25. SAME AS EVER
26. SAME AS EVER (Instrumental)

The music on the companion compact disc is performed by Ian Whitcomb with his various bands and orchestras. As well as singing, Ian plays ukulele, accordion, and piano---except where indicated. We are grateful to ITW Industries, Inc. for permission to use these recordings. We are also grateful to Loup-Garous Productions for Track 2, part of a CD centennial salute to Rosy McHargue, who inspired and encouraged so many of us that work in the field of vintage music.

Once again I have Tex Wyndham to thank for providing me with rare sheet music covers from the period. And also Janet Klein, leader of her Parlor Boys, who has dug up some fascinating photos of "Ukulele" Al Brown and his contemporaries.

1 2 3 4 5 6 7 8 9 0

Visit us on the Web at www.melbay.com — E-mail us at email@melbay.com

Contents

Songs Of The Roaring Twenties

Songs Of "Ukulele" Al Brown

About The Author (And His Love Of Uke)

Ian Whitcomb, born in England in 1941, has been obsessed with pop songs ever since childhood. First he just sang without benefit of accompaniment. Then, in the 1950s, he discovered a cheap ukulele at his cousin's house and soon taught himself to strum and to read the uke chord shapes which were still printed in most pop sheet music.

At school and on long car rides he amused his friends and family with song and story until they cried out, "Stop!". But the conquest of Rock & Roll put the greatest stop to his ukulele music. Like the accordion (another of Ian's chosen instruments), the uke was banished to cobweb corner to lie forlorn with the unhip and the uncool until The Second Coming.

At Trinity College, Dublin, in the early 1960s, Ian became a part of The British Invasion when a recording he made, between lectures, shot into the American Top Ten chart in 1965: "You Turn Me On".

Seizing the opportunity to turn on America to sunny songs of substance, Ian took his Martin ukulele on rock bus tours throughout the United States, amusing his fellow stars — who encouraged him to record with the dear little thing. This he did:

"Where Did Robinson Crusoe Go With Friday on Saturday Night?" reached the Top Ten on the West Coast in late 1966, and "bubbled under" at #101 on the Billboard national "Hot One Hundred". Not a bad start. Ian's uke was heard on "Shindig", an ABC network show, and seen on Dick Clark's "Where The Action Is" and "The Pat Boone Show". After this he never looked back — rock had renounced him and he, in turn, renounced rock — and now he strode on regardless, waving his Ukie before him, a John the Baptist of Strummers.

From the late 1960s until now (and the future) he has continued to record — and to write about — the sturdy old songs of Tin Pan Alley. Almost all his discs have featured his ukulele; he has played it on network TV shows such as "Today", "Tonight" and "Tomorrow", " Merv" and "Mike Douglas". He has taken it on stage at the Montreux Jazz Festival in Switzerland, to the consternation of Art Blakey & His Jazz Messengers; he has irritated serious ragtime fanatics at The Scott Joplin Festival in Sedalia; he has left Ukie in railway carriages and got him back hours later; he has held blackguards at bay with Ukie; he has frightened neo-Nazis, who feared its black case to be concealing a weapon. It *is* a weapon: a cultural one.

Today the battle is over: the ukulele is re-established as an instrument to be taken seriously. Ian hopes it won't be taken *too* seriously. The Great Revival is sweeping the world and Ian is proud to be part of it. Everybody with any sense is uke-crazy; there are festivals and songbooks and coffee table books; there are newfangled ukes like the Fluke (Ian owns one called "Flukie").

Lots of rock stars are taking to the uke, including Pearl Jam and Todd Rundgren. The late George Harrison was fond of bringing out the ukes at the end of an evening, rather as one would bring out the brandy and cigars. Sir Paul McCartney confirms this.

Ian has been in the forefront of the revival: appearing as a regular in Jumpin' Jim Beloff's "Uketopia" concerts at McCabe's Guitar Shop in Santa Monica. A documentary has been made of these events. Among the artistes in that film is Janet Klein, the vivacious leader of The Parlor Boys, of which Ian is now a proud member. Janet has made three CDs and is a sensation in Japan.

Recently Ian has been involved in writing and performing the music for several movies — and he has always managed to get plenty of ukulele onto the soundtrack: "Stanley's Gig" (with regular screenings on the Starz Encore channel) includes many of his songs ("Ukulele Heaven" and "The Uke Is On The March" can be found in his first Mel Bay uke book, "Ukulele Heaven"; "Dreams" is in "Uke Ballads"); "The Cat's Meow", a Lion's Gate release, directed by Peter Bogdanovich and starring Kirsten Dunst, contains over an hour of Ian & His Bungalow Boys, plus lots of uke strumming — Miss Dunst, who squeals when she sees Ukie, sings "After

You've Gone" to Ian's uke accompaniment on the end credits of the movie. Showtime has a new movie called "Last Call", set in 1940 and starring Jeremy Irons and Sissy Spacek, which has no less than thirteen original songs by Ian, and the big main ballad, "Same As Ever" is uke-based. You can hear many of these songs on the CD that accompanies this book; and then you can learn to play them.

If you'd like to know more about the author and his life in music visit www.ianwhitcomb.com. Email Ian at ianwhitcomb1@aol.com.

Ian, incidentally, is applying to be considered for the Guinness Book Of World Records: he has 23 screen credits in "The Cat's Meow."

Books By Ian Whitcomb

After The Ball: Pop Music from Rag To Rock (1972)

Tin Pan Alley: A Pictorial History (1975)

LotusLand: A Story of Southern California (1979)

Whole Lotta Shakin': A Rock 'n' Roll Scrapbook (1982)

Rock Odyssey: A Chronicle of the Sixties (1983)

Irving Berlin & Ragtime America (1987)

Resident Alien (1990)

The Beckoning Fairground: Notes of a British Exile (1994)

Treasures of Tin Pan Alley (1994)

Vaudeville Favorites (1995)

The Best of Vintage Dance (1996)

Songs of the Ragtime Era (1997)

The Titanic Songbook (1998)

Titanic Tunes: Songs From Steerage (1998)

Songs of the Jazz Age (1998)

Ukulele Heaven (1999)

Uke Ballads (2001)

For a free catalog of Ian Whitcomb products (CDs, books, videos), write to ITW Industries, Box 451, Altadena, California, 91003. Or visit Ian's website at www.ianwhitcomb.com. Listen to Ian's classic NPR radio shows at www.radiofreeworld.com

Introduction

The music in this book lay in a piano bench for decades, part of the estate of a well-to-do Pasadena widow who had willed her effects to the Huntington Library. Only recently was this music examined and, amongst the Alley sheets, I found writings not only by the widow herself but also the notebooks of one Al Brown, an itinerant performer patronized by the lady. Brown seems to provide a link between the songsters of the 19th century and the electronic entertainment which engulfed the world from the 1920s when the microphone conquered, making static what was once roving. The centuries-old minstrel odyssey was over. Now the entertainer presided from on high, as untouchable and as unknowable as a god.

The following is my interpretation of the papers discovered in that old piano bench . . . .

The Legacy of 'Ukulele' Al Brown

"I clapped my hands in glee and my eyes filled with the salt of a sweet sadness," wrote Elsie Pangland-Frosset in scribbled pencil on one of her initialed paper napkins. "How is it possible for a mere popular song to take me into such a welter of emotions?" The song, innocuous enough in itself, was "I'll Sit Right On The Moon — And Keep My Eyes On You," an amusing trifle — a conceit, really — from a far country of pleasant mustiness. But it carried some dark baggage: Elsie had danced a mad fox trot to the song at a dance back in 1913 when it was young and fresh; three months later her husband Hiram dropped without warning on the 17th green, dead before he reached the grass.

She picked up her crystal glass gamely, swirling the wine slowly, and called for more music: "Headier! Heartier!" She did not mean a Freudian march, even though this was late 1924 and such notions were in the air. She craved the hard liquor of nostalgia, she wished to be back at "The Darktown Strutters' Ball," with that exciting frisson of danger, inherent in such slumming. So Al Brown, the evening's entertainer, went into the old number with but the quickest of winks to his hostess.

Brown was getting known on local radio as "Ukulele Al" but tonight, at Mrs. Pangland-Frosset's weekly soirée of parlor music in her Pasadena mansion, he was a service provider, manning her grand piano, pumping out the old songs with reverence, leading the ladies in a singalong. It was good money and there were perks attached: some pretty tasty canapés and dips, plus imported wines courtesy of certain ships-of-good-cheer up from Mexico. Elsie might look the very pillar of Pasadena society — rigid in dress, stuck with flowers — but she sure knew how to put on a gathering. And after the ladies had left there'd be a slap-up supper of hot viands and creamy mashed potatoes in the kitchen, without any staff around to cramp his style.

Elsie — Al was allowed to call her that — had leanings towards literature. She belonged to the local Shakespeare Club (as well as several flower garden societies required of her social class) and, given the opportunity, she'd read from her notebook of musings or even from her collection of napkin jottings. She believed in spontaneity, she was modern in that way. She subscribed to "Saturday Night" because the magazine so often ran articles and photographs concerning modern dance of the free-flowing improvisational variety — willowy females in thin muslin reaching for the stars one instant and pointing to the earth the next. She followed trends in art too, and was fascinated by abstraction and, lately, mechanism.

With all this devotion to respectable culture it would appear odd that Elsie should show an indulgence for the common or garden popular song, especially the jazzy type. Odder still to hear Al Brown sing of "Dapper Dan," the colored Pullman porter and his lascivious goings from station to station, state to state — within the luxuriously appointed drawing room of Elsie's mansion.

"Rollymore," was a stone edifice in Scotch baronial set in an estate of 21 acres, paid for by her late husband Hiram with money made from decades of fruit canning in Hawaii. The drawing room had been featured in a recent edition of "House Beautiful" where much had been made in the text of the gigantic granite fireplace (big enough to house a medium-size family), the wall array of other people's crests, and the threatening but impressive galvanized steel griffins protruding from various alcoves. Conversation pieces, there is no doubt, reckoned the author of the article. But, in truth, the room and the entire mansion reflected not Elsie's taste but that of Hiram. She kept it up because she had great respect for the past. Indeed, she wished she could hold her personal history, put it in a can and freeze it forever. She herself had no interest in materialism — at least, she paid it no attention and took her creature comforts for granted — and had no regard for the latest gadgets in this increasingly electricity-obsessed age. Although, as we have mentioned, she might follow such arts movements as mechanism she had no machine music in her home; no phonograph, and no player piano. She also had no radio — Al Brown had been brought to her notice by a fellow matron.

Her piano was an exception. A machine, true, but it took blood and guts to play it. The instrument was a full-sized grand handcrafted by Broadwood of England, weighing tons, and polished so highly by her servants that she could watch, as if spying, the faces of her circle reflected in the piano's black gloss as they sat at her soiree listening to the art of Al Brown.

But, she wondered, were her friends getting as much out of the music as she? Were they moved to the marrow by the pretty tunes with their sentiments of hope, of wish fulfillment, of a belief in a better tomorrow and a yesterday of yearning, and of self-pity? Or were they there out of respect for Hiram and his millions? Were they there for the smoked salmon sandwiches, which right now Mrs. Zeigler was laying into with a vengeance?

With a flutter of her hand, as if to dismiss such awful thoughts, Elsie turned her still-pretty head, with a commotion of curls, from the mirror of the piano body to the animated figure of Al Brown as he worked his peculiar magic on "All By Myself," a song of self-pity if there ever was one. Hiram had tirelessly thundered against self-pity, calling it repellent and counter-productive. Self-pity, he thundered, was the last refuge of those who can't make it in the real world but who blame others for their lack of *oomph*. He himself had come from penury, pulling himself up by his own bootstraps, so why couldn't they? Oh, Hiram could lecture forever on self-pity, on how it removes the will and the ability to alter the lot of the complainant. Elsie had suffered his lectures for years and still shuddered at the thought even a decade after his golf course death — for she, on the contrary, was unreasonably moved by the plight of anybody, rich or poor, dog or cat, possum or raccoon. She had pity to donate in spadeloads. Pity was her middle name. She made no sense but she didn't care, so there! She was a woman of pure unrefined emotions.

Al was singing of others who make winnings in this life and of how he never even makes a gain, always chasing rainbows in vain. Elsie's body shook and then convulsed. She turned to wipe away her salty but delicious tears. What a relief to have a good cry! And yet, being a reflective person, she asked herself: can these songs bring permanent satisfaction and an end to my inner turmoil? Could it be that true happiness only comes through experience, through the ups and downs and ins and outs, the laughter and the tears, the pain and pleasure of the world outside of my Pasadena fortress?

She herself, she'd willingly admit, had lived a somewhat sheltered life — her only real excitement had been Hiram's sudden demise and even then she'd been in the club house at the time, enjoying a hand of whist. Perhaps, looking back on a pleasantish round of life (so far), she should have gotten more out of the game, should have driven an ambulance as a Red Cross nurse in the recent war — such dashing uniforms! — or helped the unemployed veterans, the nasty-faced ones who'd marched downtown Los Angeles a few years back. Or attended a meeting of the International Workers Of The World, those radicals in blue denim. There'd been a gaudy meeting recently at a hall in San Pedro where, according to the papers, a brawl had broken out when the meeting was interrupted by over-zealous patriotic sailors and Ku Klux Klan members who had smeared "Red children" with treacle and knocked radical heads together. She'd shuddered reading about the melee — holding the sweet-smelling newspaper, savoring the pulp, as she munched slowly on her breakfast toast. Distant violence and hot buttered toast were one thing. The reality was quite another.

The world outside was horrid. She felt for every victim of a traffic accident, of a marital shooting, of those killed in distant wars in, say, China. In fact, the further away the tragedy the worse she felt. Some mornings she'd wake up with a sense of foreboding: something dreadful was going to happen so she'd better watch out.

The feeling could last all day, preventing her from going out, even into her beloved rose garden, forcing her to stay in bed or to lay prostrate on a sofa with a cup of herbal tea at her side, and plenty of pets at the ready — the labrador Duffy and the angora Dolly and lots of others whose names slipped her mind. Pets, you see, were free of worry and dread and jealousy and hate. They were always loyal and never argued. They'd agree that Rosamund Beers had had no right whatsoever to park that revoltingly huge Packard outside "Rollymore" for, let's see, more than a week now. Supposedly it belonged to her visiting uncle, a furrier from New York. New money, much too new. And, it goes without saying, suspect. Surely the Beers must be Jewish? But they vehemently denied this, and they went to the Presbyterian church every Sunday.

Elsie had had words with Rosamund about the automobile matter, nasty words which she'd regretted almost as soon as they'd left her mouth. She'd been amazed by her burst of anger, amazed to realize that she'd used language not heard from her lips since her childhood in Kansas. How thin is the veneer of culture! How full of traps is the world outside! Better to stay safe from alarm within the thick walls of "Rollymore", behind thick drapes and rich old tapestries, surrounded by her pets and her songs. Songs brought vividly to life by the long and lightning fingers of her vagabond lover, Al Brown! What a beautiful touch he has on the ivories! What a magnificent sight when his hand, in an elegant flourish, lifts high off the keyboard, hovers for an instant, and then, like a hawk, comes diving for an intoxicating chord followed by a full arpeggio in which he rakes the piano up and down with no thought of tomorrow!

• • • • •

When in doubt, Al Brown was thinking, "Go chromatic", which he did fast because his mind had been wandering farther than usual. He put the blame on "I Hate To Lose You", the ballad he was currently rendering, a wartime song having nothing to do with war and with the clever subtitle: "I'm So Used To You Now". Nothing mushy about that notion! He'd known a few dames in his time who he could easily have gotten used to, especially those with culinary skills. How come, in the years he'd toured the USA, he'd never landed a dame like that, a real eye-filler with great skillet skill?

You know why, Al. Because you're always hightailing, skedaddling, never stopping to contemplate, speculate, coagulate your feelings into hard thoughts. You're a jazz baby, rolling along, here today and gone tomorrow, buried in the potter's field in an unmarked grave. "I Hate To Lose You" has some satisfying chord changes and a nice slide off the ninth, very sad somehow. But "Hate" — that's a strong word for an Alley ballad, especially in this high-class joint. Hate was a subject Al could lecture about if he had the academic credentials or could get on the chautauqua circuit. Sure, hate had been all around in his childhood in the slag heap chasms of West Virginia where the birds flew backwards to keep the coal dust out of their eyes and where blood was on his father's clothes after one of those pitched battles between the miners and the pit boss men and where there might be fried cat and hot water for supper.

His mother's old battered upright piano, a family heirloom from better days, had seen him out of the situation. It wasn't feasible for a boy with long artistic fingers, an ear for music and a mind for dreaming of places beyond the dark hills to be stuck in West Virginia. His mother had brought in other people's washing in order to pay for piano lessons from an old German teacher. When he was 16 he ran away, hopping a train for St. Louis because he'd heard that there were lots of piano players there and that they played hot music, ragtime and such, the stuff that filled you full of racing dreams and desires.

St. Louis was a perfect learning center. There were professors such as "One Eyed Bart," "Goodtime George," and "Stovepipe Slim." He'd just missed "Jelly Roll" Morton but he was assured Jelly would be round again sometime soon. All these teachers he watched carefully as he waited tables or slung beer in saloons and sporting houses; they lacked good manners and fine speech but they could coax a new kind of lingo out of the most injured of pianos. In fact, the more out-of-tune the instrument the stranger and more exciting the sound.

On these ramshackle music boxes young Al discovered little urchin notes that had hitherto been left alone, hiding between the cracks dividing the keyboard. Here was a world a trillion miles removed from standard, respectable America. Here was a rough and rude world—really an underworld— ready to take on all comers. Here, amidst painted women and armed sporting men, Al was to win his spurs, learning to crush two notes together and then separate them and slide them off to someplace else, producing an attractive whine like a bullet ricocheting off a rock, an effect that a classical music professor would, under duress, have termed as ornamentation of an unnatural kind, an illegal dissonance not covered by an Italian name. And yet, as Al learned when he tried out these new tricks in a public place, the effect was to delight the customers, transporting them momentarily into a land of danger and the next moment back onto the safe track of melody. This was called jazzing it up, but you had to be sparing with the blue phrases in case you upset the customers.

"Pretty Baby," the lively, jog-trotting number he was currently exercising, had been birthed in the twilight of a bawdy house, so said Al's jazz professors. But now here we are almost ten years later and "Pretty Baby" is just a sweet perennial, perfect for Elsie's drawing room, complementing the scent of roses and jasmine and fancy lace from old, old Belgium. What a long journey! What great and numerous services could a hit song provide! What kind of thrill did these classy ladies get from "Pretty Baby?" Al's fingers walked and skipped over the keys like the good pros they were. He could even recite the lyrics and play the tune at the same time, a very difficult feat as any old-timer will tell you. And he could roam in his mind too. He was in a roaming mood tonight for some reason.

From St. Louis he'd wandered around the hinterland, picking up gigs here and there in saloons, in cafes, in barrelhouses. Eventually he holed up for a long spell in Chicago due to his landing a very nice position as a "song demonstrator" with the local branch of Shapiro-Bernstein, a successful New York pop publishing outfit. The offices were directly above a chop suey joint which was useful if you were romancing a client beyond the performing of the songs. It was at the office that he met James V. Monaco, a genuine hit-maker. He was in town on a plug tour of his latest song, "If We Can't Be The Same Old Sweethearts ... Then We'll Just Be The Same Old Friends." Like his hit ballad "You Made Me Love You ... I Didn't Want To Do It," the new number had an ace melody, really flowing and with poignant little turns at the right moment.

The great man was dressed expensively in a Paris suit of silk with matching silk handkerchief falling beautifully from the breast pocket. He was long way from his early days in Chicago as Ragtime Jimmie, piano pounder in blood and guts saloons. Al was thrilled to demonstrate the new song in front of the composer and afterwards Jimmie gave him a few tips on accompaniment, telling him to lay off the octave ragtime in favor of thumbing, which meant using the left hand thumb to emphasize the tenth of a chord while the right hand fills in the rest of the chord. This technique, said Jimmie, left you free to sell the song vocally and if you needed to stress a lyric all you had to do was to let the right hand play the melody while you declaimed like a an orator on a soap box. Al took serious note of all this invaluable advice and dedicated himself for the next year to learning his trade.

Then came The Great War. We can't get into Al's mind about what he did in The Great Adventure. He never brought up the subject in public and seems to have shut it behind a steel door in his memory. Was he a spy? Was he a radical? Did he become a Red? He certainly came to display plenty of knowledge about the Wobblies and their ways at Elsie's "Current Affairs" parties which she held every other month, as an alternative to the house concerts. At the parties he'd regale the ladies with tales of union organizing in the logging camps and fruit fields of the west. Of course, Al was quick to explain that he'd been present simply as an entertainer. But then he'd proceed to roar with laughter as he told how, at one big logging camp, the Wobblies had complained about the rough carbolic soap provided in the workers' washroom and had demanded and received twelve boxloads of the same fancy scented soap found in the management washroom. Straight away the men were disgusted by the expensive soap because it wouldn't wash off pitch. They threw the rest of the boxes into a heap outside the management's main office. But understand, Al would say dramatically, the boys were one up on the bosses, they'd got their way, they'd disrupted the system! And his laughter would turn to a cackle, to almost an eery keening. Some of the ladies grew frightened but Elsie would later reassure them that Al Brown was only play-acting, that it was all in fun.

However, there were times when Elsie was alone with Al and when too much liquor had been provided and Al would grow ornery, picking quarrels for no reason and begging Elsie to duke it out with him. She'd quickly direct him to the piano where he'd work off these tiresome bouts of contrariness by punching out the dirtiest licks ever heard.

Immediately after the war Al was back in Chicago working once again as a song plugger. Now, in the early 1920s, at the very start of the Jazz Age, radio had started making some noise — not just with jazz music but with the noise of money. Oh, it could come jingling down, the radio people soon realized, if you used a little zippy music (tempered with some lullaby ballads) to draw in the listeners and once you'd done that — zap! — you had them like a fairground barker and you could sell them anything. Al and his fellow song pluggers quickly realized that radio could be another outlet for song plugging. Radio was ravenous for music. So Al started pioneering forth from the office, armed with the latest sheets, to invade the radio stations and offer to perform on the air at once and for free. What a deal! Al would play the piano and deliver his material into a table microphone sitting right there in front of him on the lid of the instrument. Al wasn't a bit afraid of the mike, like so many of these stentorian-voiced operatic singers were. No, he made love to the mike, murmuring his songs in a dulcet tone, getting closer and closer to this black tin altar, worshipping with respect, and every husk in his voice getting picked up and conveyed to wherever — farms, mansions, city hall, you name it. He developed a very nice act and boy did the mail come in! Especially from the ladies, the lonely ones, the shut-at-home ones.

Soon the old wanderlust got into him and he suggested to the sales manager of his publishing house that he take his act out on the road, roaming from burg to burg, hitting each and every radio station, a traveling song salesman, a new kind of troubadour. Whatever sells songs, said the boss. And off went Al.

Well, the midwest and the rural folk were one thing — an easy mark and full of farm hospitality and ham and eggs — but the big cities were another. They'd seen it all, they'd seen other radio pluggers like Al. Arriving in Los Angeles in 1924, after a hard slog in the East where he found his folksy style was considered cornball, he decided to take some time off by looking around, taking in the city and its ways. It seemed to be a whole bunch of cities. Well, more like a strung-out collection of villages. Of course, the newspapers touted Los Angeles as a big deal in every way. To Al, downtown in a modest rooming house, the place was just a larger version of the hick towns he'd conquered, the same overall cheapness, the cheap stores, the cheap people. The rich were cheap too, only with a gloss of paint over their essential tattiness.

Los Angeles was like one of its celebrated palm trees — exotic and exciting seen on the horizon at sunset, but when you got close and inspected, your hands would be covered in ooze and dirt and there'd be a funny smell. Yes, Al was suffering from the newcomer's inferiority complex. He wasn't in the movie business or in oil, so he got no respect. Why, even when he played a nifty new song on the piano in the rooming house nobody gave him time of day. There were too many movie posters. He didn't like it. He didn't have any angles on the movies.

He'd heard about how really important dance bands played the hotel and that they were a good new plug for songs. But as luck would have it he didn't need to even open his briefcase of song samples: the hotel was offering a Ladies Excuse Me night — meaning that women could invite men to dance — and before he could reach the bandstand to talk to the leader he was accosted by a middle-aged lady and asked to step the upcoming waltz with her. He looked her up and down and knew she meant money. The precious stones were everywhere, even in her hair. Yes, she was a little old for dalliance but Al sensed an interesting relationship in the offing.

During the dance — and the subsequent ones and then the late supper — Mrs. O.K. Lyon talked about divorce and how useful it was in getting rid of O.K. because after all it was her front office manner that got the customers into the guts of the store, in the back, where O.K., with his grimy fingers and runny nose, could supply them with all the necessary plate condensers, teledyne tubes, all the stuff you needed to build a radio. Yes, he'd been early in the game, but he was a backroom boy. She was the sales pitcher, and now the O.K. Lyon stores were all over the West. She deserved his money. And anyway, she'd caught him with a movie extra, some green girlie up from Georgia, and that was that, if you had an ace lawyer and boy did she have one!

Al was a good listener and immediately he heard the radio word his ears pricked up. Thoughtfully he stirred his coffee. The last dance was a waltz, "Wonderful One," and Al took the opportunity to sing along with the music. "Hey, you're pretty good," said Mrs. Lyon, pushing him back to regard him more carefully. "Are you in the business?" "I thought you'd never ask," said Al, with a smile to counter the underlying seriousness.

By around midnight Mrs. O.K. was cooing at him and he was calling her Madge. She said she kept a special bottle in her room and would he help her empty it. Did she live in the hotel? No, she replied, she lived in Santa Barbara, such a tasteful spot and far from commerce. She was here to see her daughter. And what did her daughter do, if anything? "She takes after me. I tried to stop her, said she could live with me, but she's independent, you see, like me. She's the program director at KFI, a radio station." Al was really getting interested now. "And I'd so hoped she'd leave that dirty business behind!"

Now, please don't assume that Al was predatory, a lounge lizard. He never made the first move; he was just genuinely interested in what older women had to say, and God bless him for that because there are a lot of females who never get a word in when the men are up and about and shouting. Women need a face to confess into, and Al was all sympathy, with buckets of pity to spare as well. So you see, Al was really performing a service for Madge, easing away her hate for O.K. and his philandering, giving her a good-time relief from the flowered boredom of Santa Barbara. Al could sear behind the surface and see that for all Madge's toughness she really needed a little loving and a receptive ear.

With one brisk phone call, Madge arranged for Al to get a meeting with her daughter Margot at KFI. Al had done his homework: he knew that KFI was a powerhouse station with plans to spread its message every which way on the ether. Life or fate was on his side and Al, a messenger from the 19th century, deserved to meet the technology of the 20th. A radio minstrel!

The morning of the meeting he dressed in his best suit—his only one actually, but he made it look like his best. He was surprised to find that KFI was stuck up on the roof of the Packard building on Flower Street He'd imagined it to be spread out on the ground, a splendid Spanish castle with grounds, like so many of the businesses in Los Angeles. But then, Al reassured himself, radio's a state of mind, a creation for stimulating the imagination.

Of course, everybody knew — and Al was soon informed — that the Packard building was the domain of Earle C. Anthony, the statewide distributor of Packard automobiles, and a go-ahead businessman of great vision and serious ties and vests. Anthony, a man from Nowheresville, had introduced neon to the Southland after seeing it at work in Paris, France. All night there glowed PACKARD from the 30 ft neon sign on top of the building and now it was flanked by two twin radio towers, 75 ft high, telling everybody that soon there would be a superstation operating from the roof, far larger and louder than before, boasting a 50000 watt capability.

Two years ago — my, but that seemed like in prehistoric times! — Mr. Anthony founded the station by setting up a 5 watt transmitter on a breadboard in his kitchen and enunciating to no-one in particular: "Hello there. This is Earl C. Anthony, owner and operator of KFI. You give us your attention and we will offer you worlds of delight and profit." In no time at all the station had gained 500 watts and had a business under-standing with a local newspaper so that you could learn that at 5.30 pm Nick Harris, retired L.A. detective, would be recounting his exploits, and at 6 pm there'd be the KFI sermon which tonight is titled, "God's Inner World And Its Moral Glow," and if you stayed up real late, beyond 10 pm, then you could enjoy Abe Lyman & His Orchestra broadcasting live from the Ambassador Hotel. Truth was, it was turning out that music attracted the most listeners (and thus customers): the letters told the story: a nurse from the La Vina Sani-tarium, up in Altadena, wrote of late night dance bands giving inspiration and succor to ailing patients with chronic breathing problems; 200 miles out at sea, a captain compliments the station on the splendid selections performed by the KFI concert orchestra; and in Sheffield, England, a lad of 16 reported that, by the magic of the nighttime ionosphere, he picked up a weak signal of jazz played by a "Gabe Wyman" at 468 wave-length. The listener clearly was referring to KFI's Abe Lyman (who also superintends the house bands, including the concert orchestra, and sometimes broadcasts to the kiddies as Uncle Nate From Old Kentucky). Mr. Anthony was a very conservative man but he knew a good deal when he saw it: if jazz sold socks, candy, and cars, then jazz it would be.

By now Al had been conveyed by the all-electric elevator up to the top of the Packard building and was safely inside the reception room of KFI, with construction workers and men in long white coats busying about all around him. It was hard to make himself understood by the pretty little piece of fluff sitting at the front desk surrounded by a bank of telephones.

Eventually she checked her appointments book and, in a piping voice, asked him to please take a seat because Miss Lyon was "tied up" at present but would see him as soon as she was free.

Al chose a tall wrought-iron chair, sat back, and pulled out a cheroot. Facing him on the wall was a huge painting, an artist's rendition of how the new superstation would look. Much of it was a bit too technical for Al's earthy brain but helpful captions explained the greatness to come: Western Electric, the builders, were installing water-cooled rectifier tubes and generators so that there'd be no more ghost tones creeping in from wall echoes as in the dark ages of radio. To Al's eyes the equipment seemed merely big and ugly. But he mar-veled at the depiction of the station's future interior design: a white marble switchboard, a generally Spanish tone in the archways and statues, relieved by a scattering of Chinese screens. "In consideration of the sensibili-ties of our performers," read a caption to a section showing a reception room filled with Italianate vases and splashing fountains and caged birds of paradise, "We have chosen surroundings with a view to the stimulation of fine art."

Already, on another wall, workers were hanging a hefty oil painting showing, in a most realistic style, the pageant of the taming of the West — well-muscled frontiersmen shaking hands with equally well-muscled redskins; genial old Spanish priests welcoming generously-proportioned dusky maidens to the door of a quaint ivy-covered mission. Al was thrilled to his marrow but, unfamiliar with both the people and the landscape, his pleasure was spoiled by regret because in all of his travels he'd never encountered anything like the contents of this painting. Were there any remnants left of such an Eden?

Al was shaken from his reflections by a sudden giant voice pounding out from behind him. He turned around but all he could see was a large blown-up photograph of a gleaming Packard with a glowing-faced gentleman at the wheel. The voice seemed to fit the driver and Al guessed this to be Earle C. Anthony. He also guessed that hidden behind the photo was a very large loudspeaker. He'd never heard such bass response in all his radio days.

"On December the ninth," declared the voice, "The mighty voice of a brand new KFI will roar from the gargantuan towers of Earle C. Anthony's business empire across the nation, to the huts of patient prospectors in Alaska, to the isolated and lonely in the mountains and deserts, and out across the ocean to ships ploughing their way to the other side of the Earth!"

Even the reception girl had stopped her fingernail work at the sound of this grand announcement. Then a man in a white coat said to another man in a white coat: "A good test, very radiophonic. The bass boost works swell." His fellow worker replied, "And how!"

A quieter voice came over the hidden speaker: "Send in Mr. Brown, please".

A small door to the right of the receptionist mysteriously opened on its own, gusting out a perfumed breeze. "Please enter", said the girl with a dismissive wave of her hand and without looking up at Al.

Margot Lyon sat straight in a high Spanish colonial chair. Spectacles hung from her neck. Her desk was long and large and immaculate. There was hardly a paper on it. From two horn speakers hanging from the ceiling there poured out the sound of a lugubrious theatre organ. Al recognized "Poor Butterfly," a big hit of a few years back. Miss Lyon picked up on his look.

"We do cater to the older audience as well as the young," she said, even as he was still walking towards her. "We are aware of the past and of its inhabitants." She smoothed down the frilly front of her creamy white shirt.

"Take a seat, Mr. Brown. My mother had good things to say about you." Al studied Miss Lyon as he settled into a somewhat smaller version of the program director's chair. She had a handsome face, rather than the pert-pretty face of her mother. He found himself directed to her eyes which were sending out radiant sparkles like messengers of strength and support. Yet, from her bearing and her severe suit, he felt she was definitely off limits. This was a gal with a head on her and screwed down tight.

"My mother also told me about your show business experience — and hopes. So let me tell you about radio as it is today. Forget about yesterday. I'm talking here and now and, most importantly, tomorrow". Al shifted in his chair so as not to betray his current feeling: a funny one at the base of his spine.

She started her speech: "It is peculiar to witness the reaction of those who hear singers in the studio and then walk out to the loudspeaker and hear the same voice as it comes off the air. A tenor, whose voice in the studio seems to lack resonance and purity, will broadcast with the utmost clarity and purity, leaving nothing to be desired"

"Whereas, Mr. Brown — if I might get your proper attention — whereas a trained voice that from the concert stage has delighted thousands, will not radiate at all. You have, I learn, experience in both the field of theatre as well as rural radio. You will appreciate, then, that here — especially here in a growing world-beating metropolis — every program must be planned as though it were being played before a theater audience with the lights off."

She granted him a test to judge his tonal possibilities. Rather than sing he decided to display his all-round entertainer skills. Also, he was getting queazy with all the technical talk and the neatness and sewn-up quality about KFI, about Los Angeles in general. So he recited a fragment he'd used once or twice on rural radio:

"I can't be what Shakespeare was, I can't do what great folk does. But, by ginger, I can be ME! And among the folks that love me, nothin' more's expected of me".

The engineer gave an OK sign, making an "O" with his thumb and first finger. Miss Lyon, inside the control booth, leaned closer, putting her spectacles on, then resting her chin on her fist. A long pause. Then: "You display folk appeal. We have a lot of immigrants from the mid-west out here." She came into the broadcasting room. "What about a song?" "What about a ukulele? Would you have a uke in so grand an emporium?" "My dear man, of course we have such an instrument! We have accordions, too. And even Jews harps. We are in the *people* business here at KFI!"

He started to play a peppy song about hot lips. "No, no!", she ordered. "No jazz. Jazz is passé, jazz is out. Give us something sweet and sentimental." He sang "Alice Blue Gown," a surefire number. Even so, he gave it strong, yet kept the performance intimate and sincere, singing for her and her alone.

She looked bothered. She took off her spectacles and gave them a good polish. She said she'd let him know.

A week later Al was hired. From his very first broadcast he was a hit. The mail poured in. It was 90% from women. Even rich ladies in Pasadena . . . .

• • • • •

From the grand piano Al noticed out of the corner of his eye that Mrs. Pangland-Frosset was indulging in her habit of hugging a piece of sheet music, heaving her bosom, sniffing the sheet and then looking up at the ceiling as if to heaven. Now was she trying to eat it? Oh dear, oh dear! We've had this display before. So he quickly went into "You're In Style When You're Wearing A Smile," because the evening needed ending and the song was his radio show sign-off number. Once she gets into such a state of ecstasy you had to beat a retreat. At least, *he'd* have to. Keep that gulf between performer and audience. Not a rule he always obeyed. Elsie had a thing about the smell, the taste of print, especially if it was a song. She liked to run her fingers up and down the sheet, feeling for any embossment and to see if the cheap primary colors of the cover would come off in her hands so that she could then stain her dress. She liked that very much. We all have our eccentricities, some odder than others.

Al envied the songwriters of whatever sheet she was clutching. He wished he'd produced something to be remembered by, something that could be held and smelled and tasted. Instead he was just another ghost of the airwaves, a voice in the night, wafting into a home to provide a cheap balm for the moment, a fleeting moment of pleasure and escape. Who would ever have and hold his radio broadcasts? Even Miss Lyon would leave behind a paper trail of correspondence and memos. Miss Lyon! Dared he ask her for a date? No, keep your distance, remember your career! But that's just it — a career with nothing to show, no legacy. Oh, to be encased in hard cover, to be in a locked bookcase. When he had enough time and peace he'd sit down and write a great novel. But what would it be about? That was a tough one. A good story, that's what he needed. He thought, "I'll make the time to write this novel if it kills me. I have fine other skills so why can't I learn writing? I mean, very few people can play and sing and smile and think deep thoughts all at one and the same time, can they?"

And there were upcoming events to look forward to, events that could sail him into real stardom, maybe the movies. They were all inked into his diary. Al had always liked to have lots of appointments, to know that there'd be few times when he'd have nothing to do, to be utterly all alone. Whenever he was gloomy he'd open up his black leather book and peruse his dates, both musical and amorous.

Next weekend marked the Great Experiment, the talk of KFI, when the imminent superstation, as a preview of big things to come, would set the record for marathon broadcasting with a 48 hour music festival from the roof, under the stars, with non-stop numbers from a special KFI radio band, pooled from all the best musicians around. A charity affair to raise money for the wayward women of Hollywood, mostly girls from outside states who'd come to town in the hopes of being discovered for the movies. Nice to be performing for a good cause – makes you feel good.

Yes, Al had been selected for the team, specifically as a contributor of whispered songs deep into the night. A special new-fangled microphone was to pick up his slightest murmur, claimed the engineers at Western Electric. Should his chin bristle scrape the new mike the effect would be to the listener as if a giant redwood was being attacked by a chainsaw. He would have to be on his very best behavior. Even though it was radio, he would wear a white tuxedo with a red carnation. Margot had decided this. She was great at business decisions. What about material? She left that up to him with the proviso that he should think nocturnal, think pacification. Perhaps he'd open with "Blue Jeans," a catchy melody and with lyrics that painted an appealing picture of life up in the mountains of the Old Cumberland.

Who was he fooling? He knew full well that life in the mountains was worse than life in the mining towns below. Stunted people, stunted lives, stained pants. But Al liked to dream ideals especially when life grew murky with too many promises to too many women. He was such a nice guy, you see, and he couldn't say no. He'd been put on earth to give folks a moment's pleasure and forgetfulness, to make believe his songs told the truth. Well, surely it was possible that somewhere there existed the right girl in front of the right cottage, ready to welcome you home after a hard day's honest but dull work? He could see it now — the golden smoke snaking up to the top of the sky as the moon rose over the mountain.

It was a picture to be framed and hung in an art gallery. And yes, he, Al Brown, was about to be immortalized like in a painting: Victor records had been hired to make a custom field recording of highlights of the radio marathon and with any luck – some careful working of Margot – he'd be featured on the disc. He'd be caught as an object for posterity. So there was some point to his life after all! And what a skilled technician he had become! Right at the climax of this thought "Blue Jeans" came to its natural end. The tale had been told, the book was now closed, the A flat tonic chord capped another lovely evening of music.

• • • • •

On Thursday, November 20, the front page of The Los Angeles Times reported the sudden death of the celebrated motion picture producer and director, Thomas Ince, following an attack of chronic indigestion while attending a yachting party off San Diego. In later editions the paper revealed that Ince had been one of several movieland celebrities (including Elinor Glyn, Charlie Chaplin, and Marion Davies) aboard the Oneida, and that the pleasure boat was owned by press baron, William Randolph Hearst, who had been hosting a birthday party for Ince. There had been several rotating dance bands on board. An elaborate sound system enabled the yacht to both receive radio broadcasts from the mainland and also to send out its own messages, even programs. Hearst also had had each cabin wired for sound with a central listening post in his stateroom.

Within days of Ince's demise rumors began to circulate that there'd been some funny business on board during the night and that maybe Ince hadn't succumbed to a surfeit of oysters but to a revolver shot through the back of his head fired by Hearst in a fit a sexual fury. The whisper was that Hearst had caught either Ince or Chaplin having cabin sex with the press baron's mistress Marion Davies. It was dark, the story went, and the radio was playing "I Was A Fool", one of the many songs performed at the KFI radio marathon. Now this number was one of WRH's favorites, never failing to make him cry.

Blinded, confused, and slightly demented, Hearst went off to fetch his revolver. Later, Ince got shot. Maybe Hearst had mistaken him for Chaplin.

Meanwhile Al, as part of his KFI job, had caught the midnight speedboat from San Diego and had joined the yacht in order to be available as a strolling musician for the cabin entertainment of the guests, if so desired. The whisper went that several of the guests who'd witnessed the murder were pensioned off by the Hearst Corporation. Was Al one? All we know is that we never hear again of "Ukulele" Al Brown. There is no record of him being aboard the yacht. There is no record in the KFI files that he was ordered to play on board. He was never called to the subsequent inquiry. He simply disappears into the air, like the radio spirit he was becoming.

If only he'd remained on the ground, on land, as the entertainer of rich and restless ladies, or even of the passing crowd in city streets, instead of succumbing to the temptations of the new world of ether and electricity.

• • • • •

Tuning

SOPRANO UKE

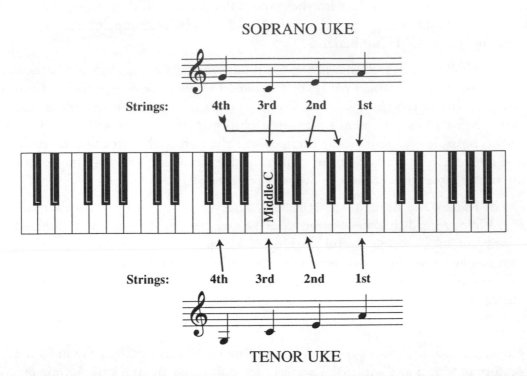

Strings: 4th 3rd 2nd 1st

Middle C

Strings: 4th 3rd 2nd 1st

TENOR UKE

Me-ow!

Words by Harry D. Kerr

Music by Mel Kaufman

CHORUS

said, _____ but   All   night long   An-go-ra   sang his   song, _____ Me -
round, _____ but   All   night long   An-go-ra   sang his   song, _____ Me -

ow, _____   Me - ow, _____ He gave   a   cab-a-ret, _____ but just one
ow, _____   Me - ow, _____ He gave   a   cab-a-ret, _____ but just one

tune he'd play, ___ Me - ow, ____ some - how, _____ Wif - ey's   long - ing
tune he'd play, ___ Me - ow, ____ some - how, _____ Folks say   death ____ and

for   com - pa - ny _____ Changed, while   he _____ sang
tax - es   are   sure, _____ But   An - go - - - ra's

on   mer - ri - ly _____ That ev - er   taunt - ing   growl, _____ That ev - er
song will en - dure, _____ When An - gel   Ga - briel blows, _____ You'll hear that

haunt - ing howl, _____ Me - ow, _____ Me - ow.   ow. _____
cat   of Joe's, _____ Me - ow, _____ Me - ow.   ow. _____

17

I'll Sit Right on the Moon

Words and Music
by Jimmie V. Monaco

see that you don't flirt, I'll see that you don't hurt an - oth - er heart so

true. And I'll come out most ev - 'ry night so I can throw down the light,__ and I will

see the things you do. So watch out and do not spoon, for I'll

sit right on the moon and keep my eyes on you.

YOU'RE IN STYLE
WHEN YOU'RE WEARING A SMILE

SONG
BY
AL. W. BROWN
GUS. KAHN
&
EGBERT VAN ALSTYNE

5

JEROME H. REMICK & Co.
DETROIT   NEW YORK

You're in Style When You're Wearing a Smile

By Al W. Brown,
Gus Kahn, and
Egbert Van Alstyne

Alice Blue Gown
(from the motion picture, "The Cat's Meow")

Words by Joseph McCarthy

Music by Harry Tierney

Slowly and tenderly

I once had a gown, it was al - most new, Oh, the
The lit - tle silk worms that made silk for that gown, Just

dain - ti - est thing, it was sweet A - lice Blue; With___ lit - tle for - get - me - nots
made that much silk and then crawled in the ground, For there nev - er was an - y - thing

placed here and there, When___ I had it on,___ I walked on the air. And it
like it be - fore, And I don't dare to hope there will be an - y more. But it's

wore, and it wore, and it wore,___ Till it went and it wasn't no more.___ In my
gone 'cause it just had to be___ Still it wears in my mem - o - ry.___

Refrain. Valse moderato

sweet lit - tle A - lice blue gown,_____ When I first wan - der'd

28

down in-to town_____ I was both proud and shy, As I felt ev-'ry

eye, But in ev-'ry shop win-dow I'd primp, pass-ing

by; Then in man-ner of fash-ion I'd frown._____ And the

world seemed to smile all a-round_____ Till it

wilt-ed I wore it, I'll al-ways a-dore it, My

sweet lit-tle A-lice blue gown._____

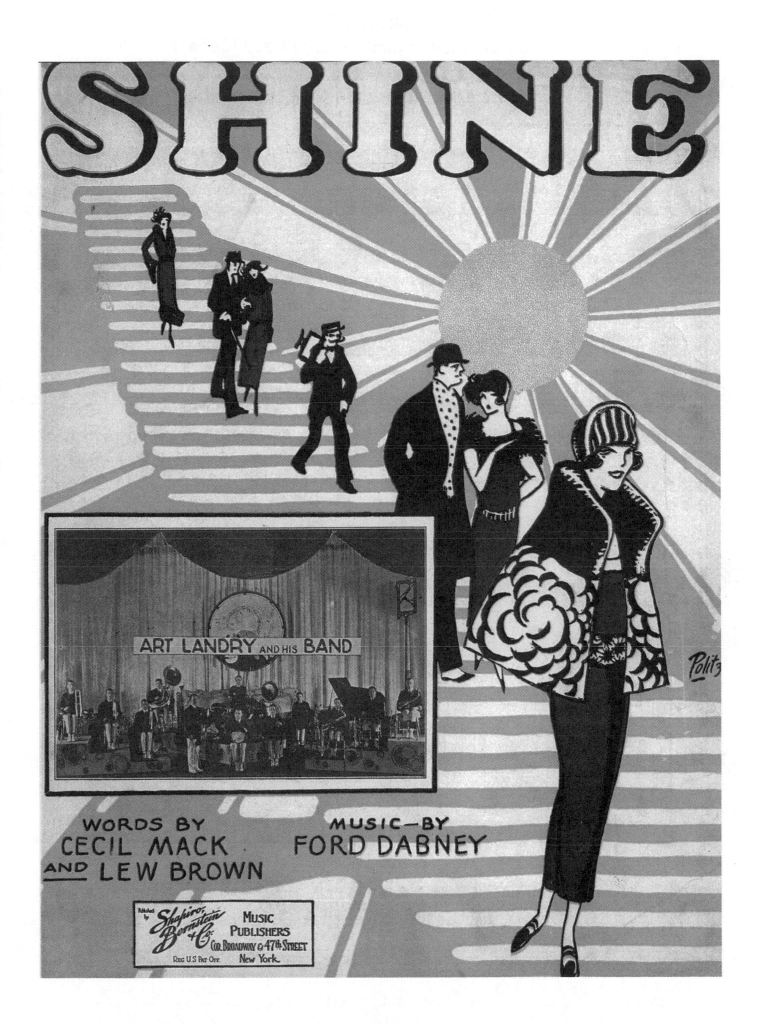

Shine
(from the motion picture, "The Cat's Meow")

Words by Cecil Mack
and Lew Brown

Music by Ford Dabney

Moderato

Eb

Shine_____ a - way your blues - ies,_____

Eb

Shine,_____ start with your shoes - ies_____

G7   Cm

Shine each place up, make it look_____ like new,

F7   Bb7

Shine your face up wear a smile_____ or two,

Eb

Shine_____ your these and thos - ies_____

32

You'll find that ev - 'ry - thing will turn out fine,

Folks will shine up to____ ya, Ev - 'ry-one will

how - dy - do____ ya, You'll make the whole world

1. shine.

2. shine.____

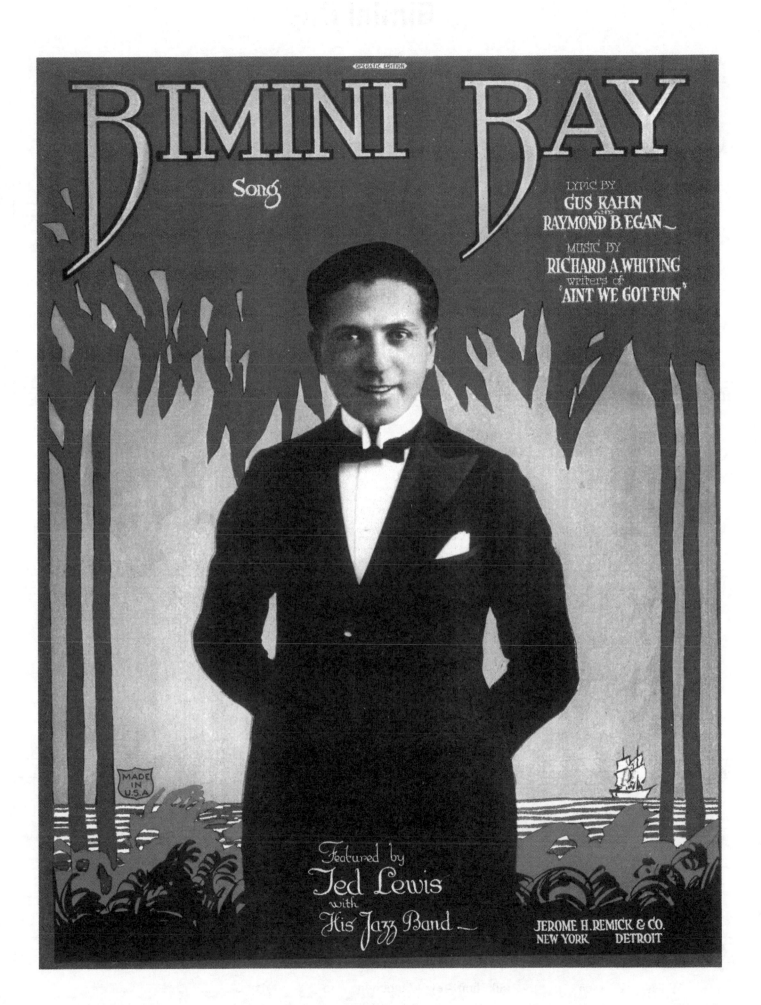

Bimini Bay

Words by Gus Kahn
and Raymond B. Egan

Music by Richard A. Whiting

Gad - a - bouts   of   now - a - days   All   spend their wint - er
There is mag - ic   in the moon That   makes De - cem - ber

hol - i - days____ Way   down   old Bim-in - i   way_____
seem like June____ Way   down   old Bim-in - i   way_____

Men of Wall   street   big and haught - y   Grow a tri - fle
Count the stars if   you are a - ble   In the skies or

gay and naught - y   Way down   on Bim-in - i   Bay_____
on a la - bel   Way down   on Bim-in - i   Bay_____

When   men   talk hon - ey - moon-ing to - day_____
Palm   trees   wav - ing so friend-ly at   you_____

Where the Green Riv-er   flows   There we'll spend our days   And we'll try to raise
Down on Bim - in - i   Bay   And   of late I've heard   Ev - 'ry wise old bird

Tom and Jer - ries who knows   Each night we'll sam - ple our pri - vate stock
Will   be fly - ing that way   You'll find that's where the good law - yers are

Wind up the   cat and put out   the clock   Oh   by Jim - in - y
And how they   prac-tice at ev - 'ry bar   Oh   by Jim - in - y

won't you come with me   Down to Bim - in - i   Bay
how I'd love to be   Down on Bim - in - i   Bay_____

38

I AIN'T GOT NOBODY MUCH

WORDS BY
ROGER GRAHAM
MUSIC BY
SPENCER WILLIAMS

CRAIG and COMPANY
ROGER GRAHAM, MGR.
145 NORTH CLARK ST. CHICAGO, ILL

I Ain't Got Nobody Much

Words by Roger Graham

Music by Spencer Williams

Jazzily

There's a say - ing go - ing 'round,___ And I be - gin to think it's
If I on - ly had some - one___ That I could on - ly call my

true,___ It's aw - ful hard___ to love some - one___ When they don't care___ 'bout
own,___ For I would mar - ry them at once___ And take them to___ my

you; Once I had___ a lov - in' man,___ As
home; Ev - 'ry night___ I sigh and cry,___ No

good as an - y in this town,___ But now I'm sad___ and
hap - pi - ness at all I find,___ I have no one___ to

lone - ly, For he's gone and turned me down.___ 'Cause
love me, No one to con - tent my mind.___ 'Cause

Pretty Baby

Words by Gus Kahn

Music by Tony Jackson
and Egbert Van Alstyne

THE LADIES MAN
DAPPER-DAN
FROM DIXIE LAND
Featured with terrific Success by
Eddie Cantor
in the
"Midnight Rounders"
Music by
ALBERT VON TILZER
Lyric by
LEW BROWN
BROADWAY MUSIC CORPORATION
WILL VON-TILZER PRESIDENT
145 WEST 45TH ST. NEW YORK
MADE IN U.S.A.
6

Dapper Dan

Written by Lew Brown

Composed by Albert Von Tilzer

Snappily

1. Dapper Dan___ was a Pull-man por-ter man On a train that ran thro'
2. Dapper Dan___ was a ve-ry hand-y man On a train that ran thro'

Dix - ie. Ev - 'ry one knew Dap-per Dan,___ Knew him for a la-dies man.___
Dix - ie. Made the beds and ev-'ry - thing,___ All you had to do was ring.___

Nev-er cared___ to set-tle down,___ Had a gal in ev-'ry town. On the
If the train___ stopped an-y - where There'd be some gal wait-ing there. He'd say

train the whole day long You'll hear him sing this song_____
"This is one of mine, And there's oth-ers down the line._____

CHORUS

"If I lose my gal in Ten-nes-see_____ That won't wor - ry
"If I lose my gal in Bal-ti - more_____ That won't make me

48

C7   D7

I   ain't   hand - some,   I   ain't   sweet,___ But   I   got   a brand   of lov - in' that
won't   let   no   gal   run   my   life___ 'Cause   if   I   lose   them all   I've still

A♭7   C   D7   G7

can't   be   beat,___ I'm   the   la - dies'   man___ from   dear   old   Dix - ie -
got   my   wife,___ I'm   the   la - dies'   man___ from   dear   old   Dix - ie -

C   C7   F   Fm   C   C♯°   G7   C   C7   F   Fm   C

1.   2.

land."_____   "If   I   land."_____
land."_____   "If   I   land."_____

50

POOR BUTTERFLY

THE BIG SHOW

At the New York
HIPPODROME
Management Charles Dillingham

Staged by **R. H. BURNSIDE**
Lyrics by **JOHN L. GOLDEN**
Music by **RAYMOND HUBBELL**

T. B. HARMS
AND
FRANCIS, DAY & HUNTER
NEW YORK

Poor Butterfly

Words by John L. Golden

Music by Raymond Hubbell

taught her how to love in the 'Mer - i - can way, To love with her soul! 'twas
nev - er love a - gain she is his_____ for aye. Through all of this world, For

ea - sy to learn; Then he sailed a - way with a prom - ise to re - turn.
a - ges to come, So her face just smiles, tho' her heart is grow - ing numb.

CHORUS

Poor But - ter - fly!_____ 'neath the blos - soms wait - ing_____ Poor But - ter -

fly!_____ For she loved him so._____ The mo - ment

pass in - to hours_____ The hours_____ pass in - to years_____ and as she

smiles through her tears,_____ She mur - murs low,_____ The moon and

53

I'll Stand Beneath Your Window Tonight and
Whistle

Words and Music by Jerry Benson,
Jimmie McHugh and Georgie Price

Sassily

1. I'm all smiles, great big smiles, Just got an ans-wer to a let-ter I wrote_____ She said "Yes" "I'll be dressed" And all I did was drop her this lit-tle note and told her

2. She's some gal, some real pal We start-ed right off to the preach-er on time_____ Tied the knot On the spot And all be-cause I dropped her this lit-tle line and told her

CHORUS

I'll stand be-neath your win-dow to-night_____ and whis-tle

Whistle

for you_____ Don't hes-i-tate to

56

Wonderful One

Paul Whiteman's Sensational Waltz Hit ~

Words by
Dorothy Terriss
Music by
Paul Whiteman and
Ferdie Grofé
Adapted from a Theme by
Marshall Neilan

Sung by
JOHN MᶜCORMACK
VICTOR RECORD   NO. 961

*"You can't go wrong
With any 'FEIST' song"*

POPULAR   EDITION
LEO. FEIST INC. NEW YORK
CANADA, LEO. FEIST, LIMITED, 193 YONGE ST. TORONTO.
FRANCIS,DAY & HUNTER, 138-140 CHARING CROSS ROAD, LONDON,E.W.

Wonderful One

Words by Dorothy Terriss
Melody by Marshall Neilan

Arranged by Paul Whiteman
and Ferdie Grofé

low._____ My won-der-ful one, When ev-er I'm dream-ing, Love's

love-light a gleam-ing, I see,_____ My won-der-ful one, How my

arms ache to hold dear, To cud-dle and fold near to me,_____ Just

you on-ly you, In the shad-ow-y twi-light, In sil-ver-y

moon-light there's none_____ Like you, I a-dore you, my

life I live for you My won-der-ful, won-der-ful one._____

Margie

Lyric by Benny Davis

Music by Con Conrad
and J. Russel Robinson

get your prom - ise to me,_____ I have bought a home and ring and ev - 'ry thing, for Mar - - - gie_____ You've been my in - spir - a - tion, Days are nev - er blue;_____ Af - ter all is said and done, There is real - ly on - ly one_____ Oh! Mar - gie, Mar - gie, it's you."_____ "My lit - tle you"_____

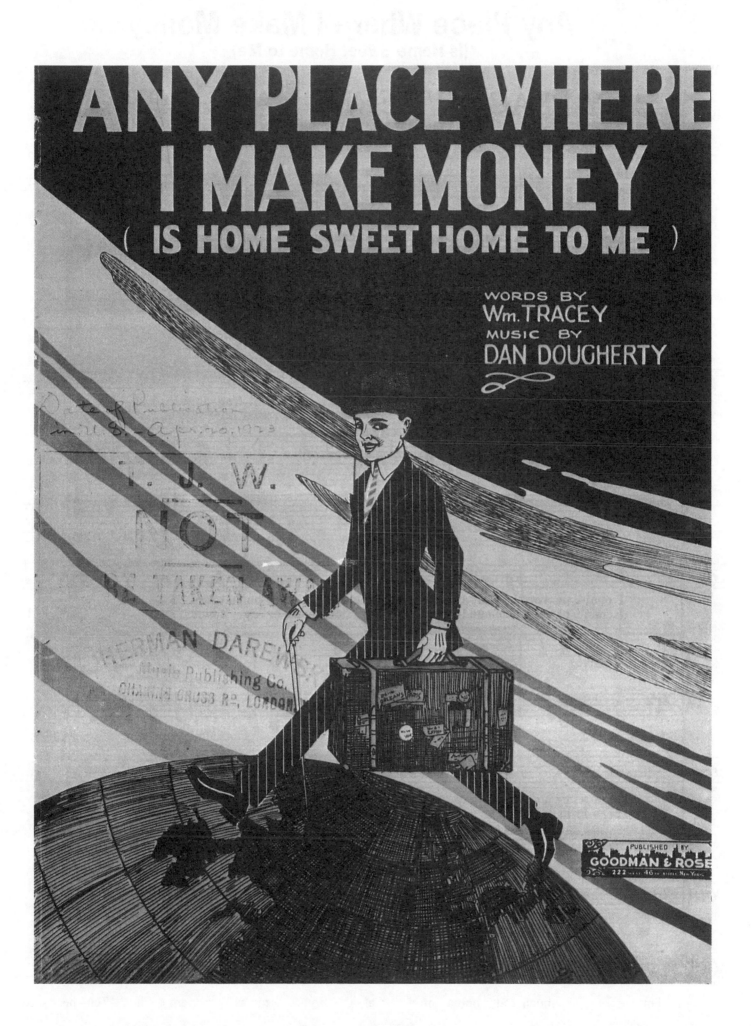

Any Place Where I Make Money
(Is Home Sweet Home to Me)

Words by William Tracey

Music by Dan Dougherty

If there's a wel - come writ - ten on the mat_____ That's the place I hang my coat and hat._____ I've lived in towns where the lights are bright, And they ne - ver think it's late,_____ And in burgs where they pull in the side - walks Ev' - ry night at half past eight._____ Oh, I wish I had some - bo - dy wait - ing but I'm just a roll - ing stone_____ And Home Sweet Home is just a mel - o - dy.

Now There are ma - ny things that you can
The town may be a small one and the
Love means more than mon - ey some poor

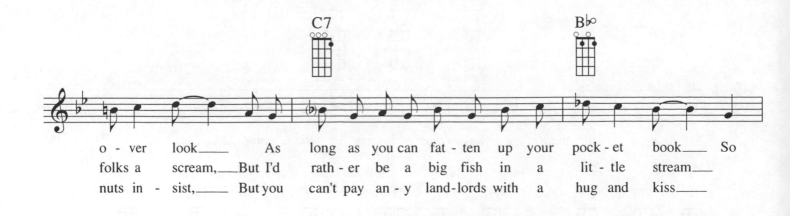

o - ver look___ As long as you can fat - ten up your pock - et book___ So
folks a scream,___ But I'd rath - er be a big fish in a lit - tle stream___
nuts in - sist,___ But you can't pay an - y land-lords with a hug and kiss___

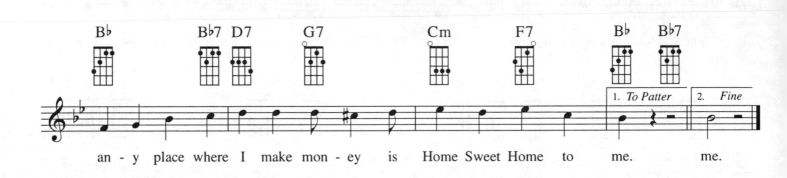

an - y place where I make mon - ey is Home Sweet Home to me. me.

PATTER
4 times

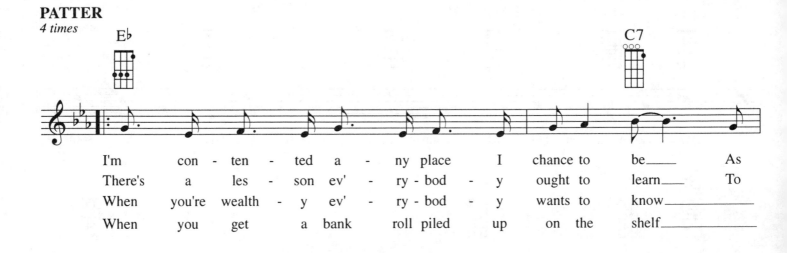

I'm con - ten - ted a - ny place I chance to be___ As
There's a les - son ev' - ry-bod - y ought to learn___ To
When you're wealth - y ev' - ry-bod - y wants to know___
When you get a bank roll piled up on the shelf___

long as I get plen - ty of the do ray me.___
keep a dol - lar out of ev' - ry two you earn.___
What you do and how you came to make your dough.___
Step right out and start in to en - joy your - self.___

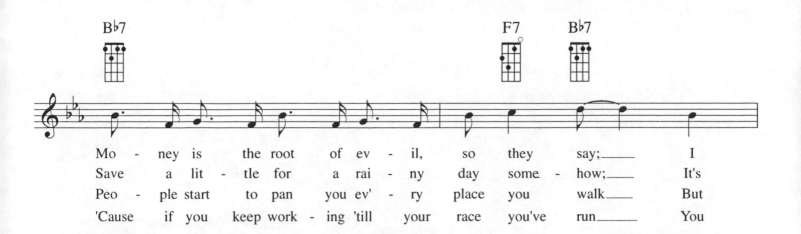

Mo — ney is the root of ev - il, so they say;____ I
Save a lit - tle for a rai - ny day some - how;____ It's
Peo - ple start to pan you ev' - ry place you walk____ But
'Cause if you keep work - ing 'till your race you've run____ You

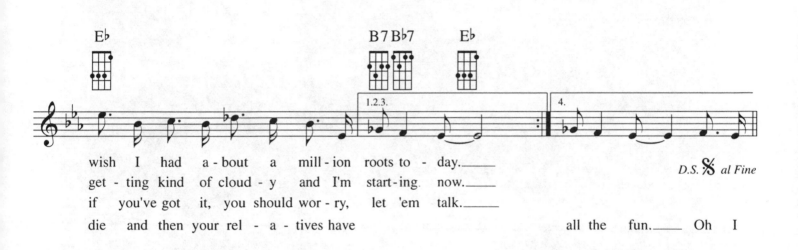

wish I had a - bout a mill - ion roots to - day.____
get - ting kind of cloud - y and I'm start - ing now.____
if you've got it, you should wor - ry, let 'em talk.____
die and then your rel - a - tives have all the fun.____ Oh I

D.S. %̸ al Fine

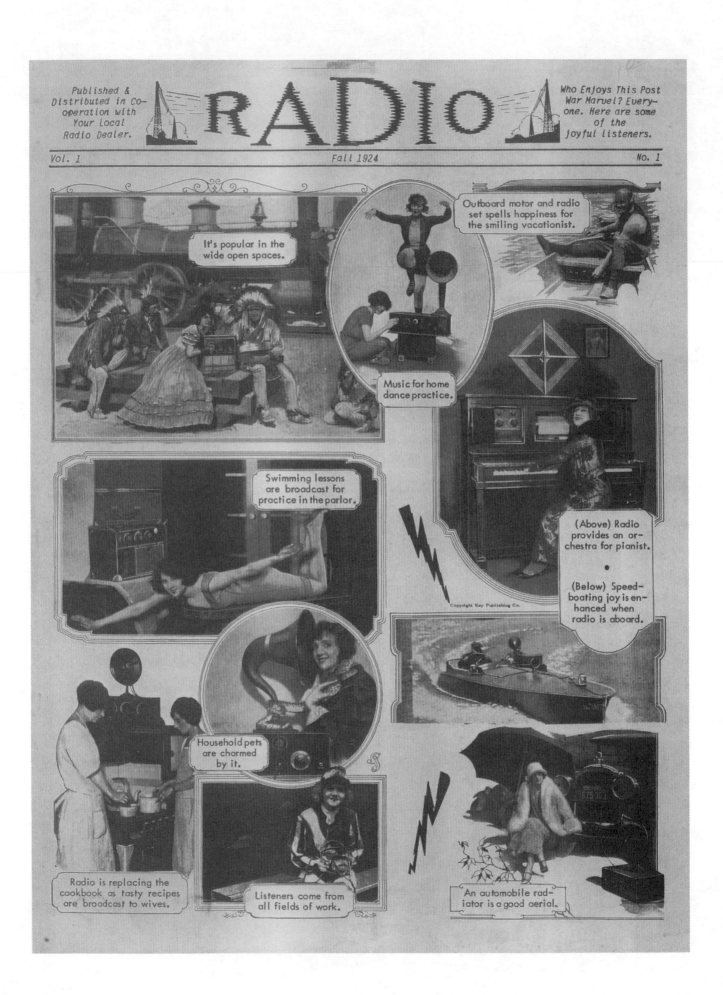

All by Myself

Words and Music by Irving Berlin

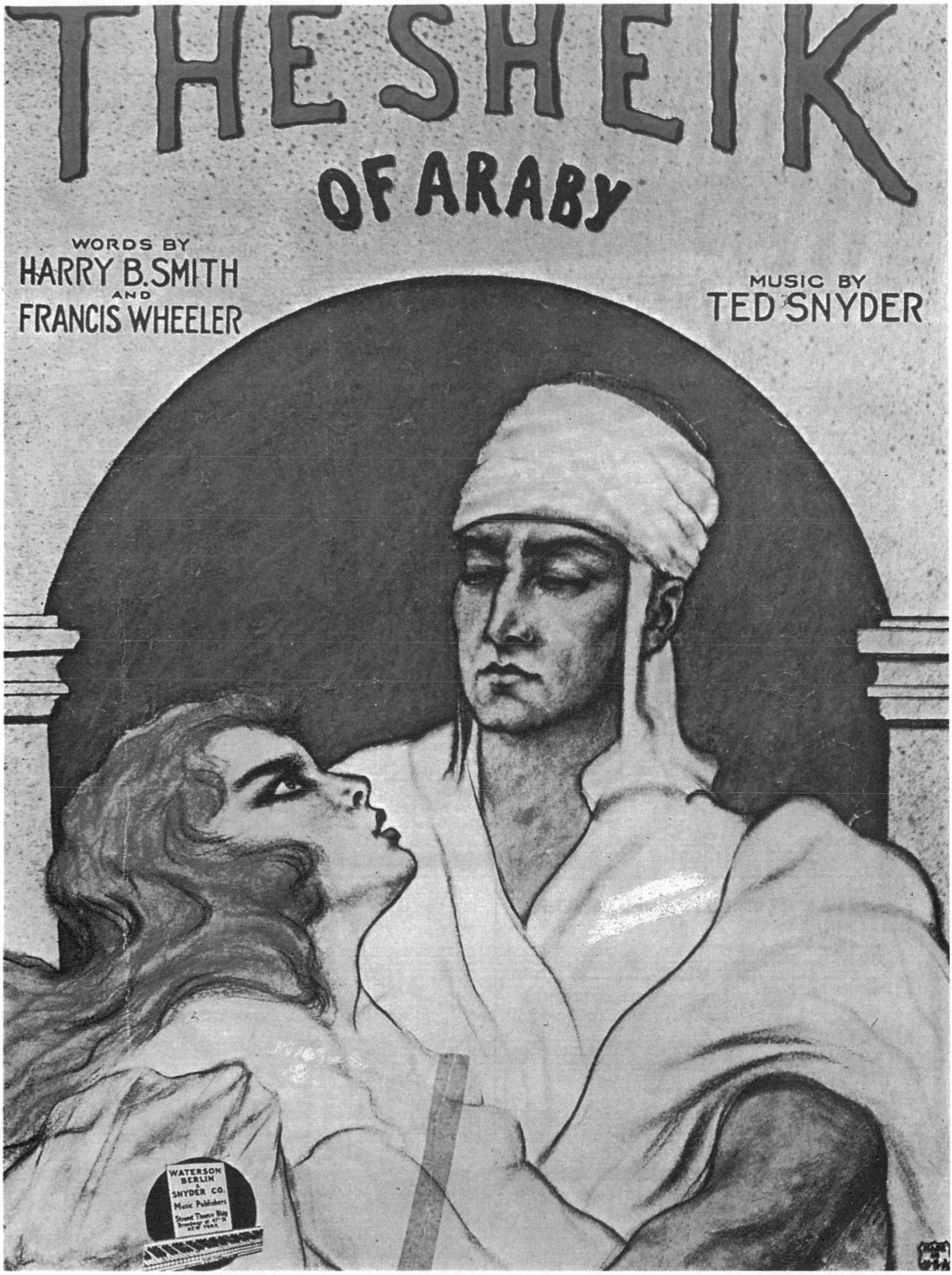
THE SHEIK
OF ARABY
WORDS BY
HARRY B. SMITH
AND
FRANCIS WHEELER
MUSIC BY
TED SNYDER
WATERSON BERLIN & SNYDER CO.
Music Publishers

The Sheik of Araby

Words by Harry B. Smith and Francis Wheeler

Music by Ted Snyder

CHORUS

79

PRICE
SIXTY
CENTS

I Was a Fool

Words and Music by Manny Romanz

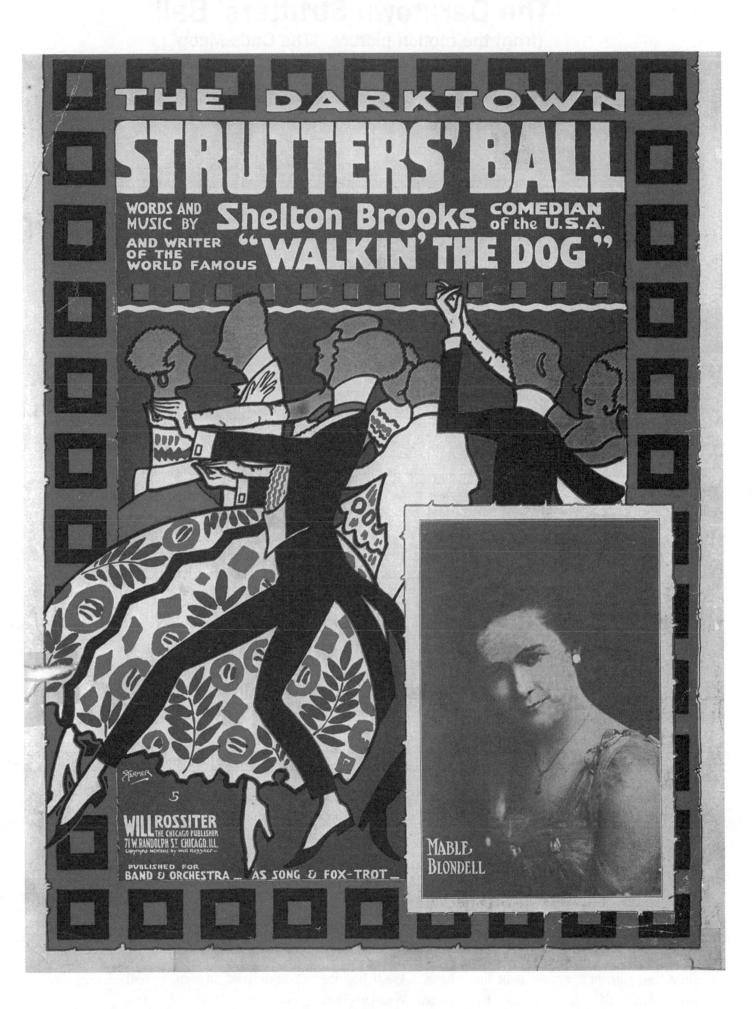

The Darktown Strutters' Ball

(from the motion picture, "The Cat's Meow")

Words and Music by Shelton Brooks

84

The Songs of "Ukulele" Al Brown

The Candyland Christmas Ball
(from the motion picture, "Last Call")

Words and Music by Al Brown

Cheekily

Gm D7

1.'Twas the night be - fore   Christ - mas   all   the   kids were a -
2.Tom - my saw what was   hap - p'ning   and   jumped in - to the

Gm D7

sleep   'cept for poor Tom - my   Tuck - er   he   was pound - ing the
breach   start - ed res - cu - ing   can - dy   ev - 'ry - thing with - in

Gm G7 C7

street   'Round the cor - ner Tom - my sees a   can - dy   shop
reach   Geor - gie Por - gie wad - dled up and said "What's   this?"

F7 B♭ Gm

peeps in - to   the win - dow and his   eyes go pop!   What a   treat   for his
Tom - my knocked him out with just one   can - dy kiss   All   the swee - ties said

E♭7(♭5) A7 Dm

tum - - my   what a won - der - ful   dream.
"Thank   you!"   "Eat us af - ter the   ball!"

87

Lonely
(from the motion picture, "Last Call")

Words and Music by Al Brown

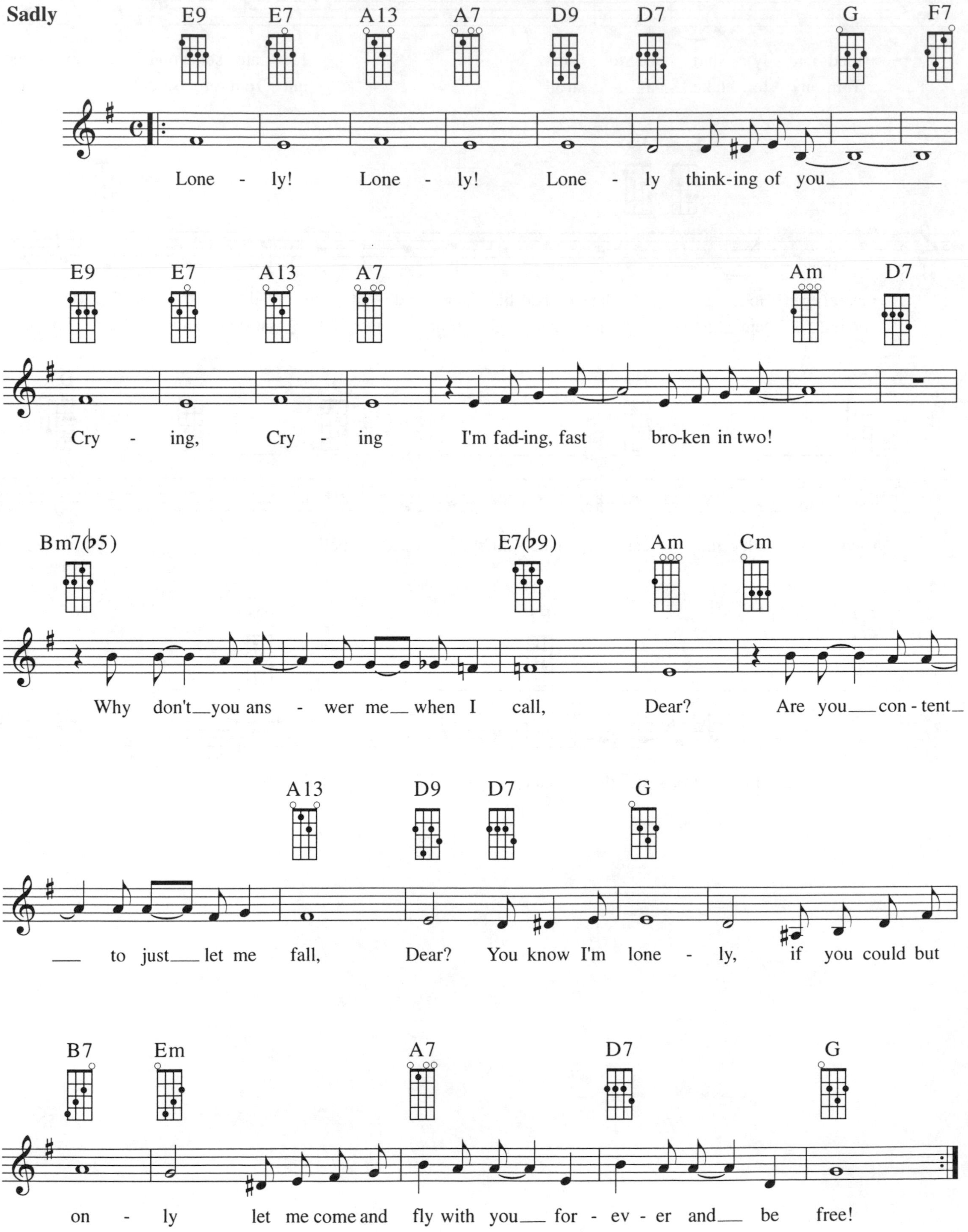

Sadly

E9 E7 A13 A7 D9 D7 G F7

Lone - ly! Lone - ly! Lone - ly think-ing of you___

E9 E7 A13 A7 Am D7

Cry - ing, Cry - ing I'm fad-ing, fast bro-ken in two!

Bm7(b5) E7(b9) Am Cm

Why don't__you ans - wer me__when I call, Dear? Are you__con - tent__

A13 D9 D7 G

___ to just__let me fall, Dear? You know I'm lone - ly, if you could but

B7 Em A7 D7 G

on - ly let me come and fly with you__ for - ev - er and__ be free!

90

When You're There
(from the motion picture, "Last Call")

Words and Music by Al Brown

A-lone a-gain and on the street, Babe. I'm feel-ing down and in-com-plete, Babe.

I know ex-act-ly what's wrong I'll tell you in this song___ When you're

CHORUS

there you make me feel so fine When you're

there I get a cer-tain sign That you

love me the same as I love you

Do I Love You? Yes I Do!

Words and Music by Al Brown

Sweetly

Down on the Farm

Words and Music by Al Brown

Rusticly

Ur - ban man born in your car____ Hark - en what I've____

____ got to say Do you find fluff in your trou - ser cuff?____

____ Do you munch your lunch____ off a tray? Tired of the taste____

____ of your air con - di - tion - er? Tired of pot rot____ and

old Ra - ma Krish-n - a? If this is so____ then pack up and go____

Come on and join me on the farm!

CHORUS

Cows and sheep and hors - es   meals with sev - en cour - ses
Hear the flow - ers grow - ing   as you're bu - sy hoe - ing

Down on the farm_____   peace - ful and calm_____   Cock - rel
                                                                                                              You can

wakes me at a quar - ter to five_____   Morn - ing breeze don't
see the beast - ies that cre - ate meat_____   Walk - ing talk - ing

make me shud - der Get my milk straight from the ud - der and when days are
T - bone steak - os and the stuff they put in ta - cos. Love - ly farm - er's

end - ing   gold - en skies are blend - ing   Down on the farm_____
daugh - ter will teach you things you ought - a   learn a - bout life_____

peace - ful and calm_____ Tur - keys gob - ble and
oh what a life_____ When you dine shout:

chat - ter with me_____ (Gobble! Gobble!) Nan - ny goats in - - -
"Un - chain the Cheese!"____ __ See it come_____ full of

vite me to tea_____ (Baaa!) Ev - en the bull_____ say fid - dle de dee_____ (Snort!)
mag-gots and fleas_____ Crawl to - wards_____ you quite at its ease__(Gorgonzola!)

Down on the farm_____ with me_____ _____

THAT'S HER NOW!
Words by
JACK YELLEN
Music by
MILTON AGER
With uke arr.
MADE IN U.S.A.
AGER, YELLEN & BORNSTEIN INC.
MUSIC PUBLISHERS
745-7TH. AVE.
NEW YORK
JACQUES MAYES

Hello, Good Morning, And How Do You Do?

(from the motion picture, "Last Call")

Words and Music by Al Brown

fun._____ Bid Mis - ter Blues good - bye._____

_____ Look stra - ight in - to his eye_____ and

tell him you've no_____ lim - it but the_____ sky!_____

You know there's no-thing that you can't ach - ieve._____ And

so I'm tell - ing you be - fore you leave._____ Eat! And fire your-self

(Instrumental)

up! And let's get mov - ing!

101

Same as Ever
(from the motion picture, "Last Call")

Words and Music by Al Brown

Wistfully

I'll al - ways love you just the same as ev - er

same as ev - er ev - 'ry day

Though you're gone your love lives on it seems dear

I can see you there with me in dreams dear Nev - er fear for

I'll hold you tight - ly just the same as ev - er

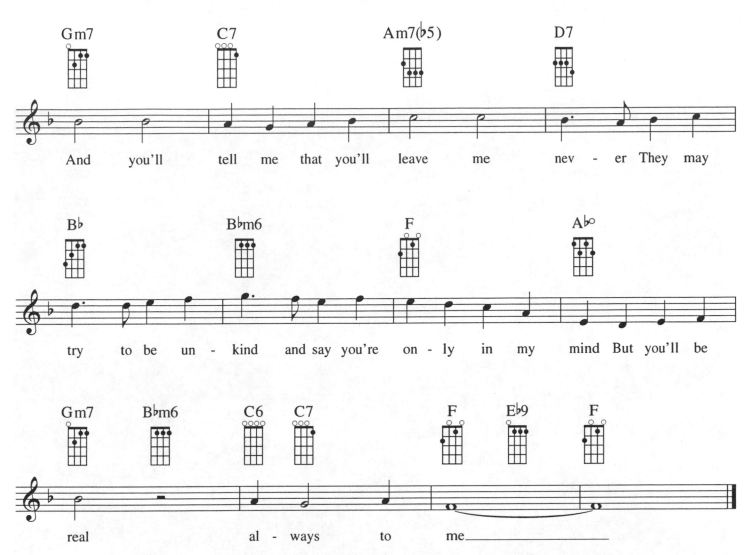

| Gm7 | C7 | Am7(♭5) | D7 |

And you'll tell me that you'll leave me nev - er They may

| B♭ | B♭m6 | F | A♭○ |

try to be un - kind and say you're on - ly in my mind But you'll be

| Gm7 | B♭m6 | C6 | C7 | F | E♭9 | F |

real al - ways to me_____

103

Ian Whitcomb and his Bungalow Boys – with Regina